THE ULTIMATE BEGINNER SERIES

ROCK GUITAR BASICS

STEPS ONE & TWO COMBINED

NICK NOLAN AND COLGAN BRYAN

M000230027

Editor/Project Manager: Aaron Stang
Cover Layout: Joann Carrera
Technical Editor: Albert Nigro
Cover Layout: Joann Carrera
Engraver: Andrew Parks

© ℗ 1995, 1996 CPP MEDIA GROUP,
a division of WARNER BROS. PUBLICATIONS
All Rights Reserved including Public Performance for Profit

CONTENTS

SECTION 1: THE BASICS
INTRODUCTION

Rock Guitar is part of the Ultimate Beginner Series. This series provides the beginner and intermediate musician with fundamental training for guitar, bass, keyboards, vocals and drums.

Rock Guitar is a stand-alone training method designed to help you build a solid foundation of technical and stylistic examples to enable you to explore all avenues of rock guitar styles. Not only will you learn the primary chords, scales, rhythm patterns and lead techniques, you will learn how to apply them. All of the examples are written in standard notation and tablature and demonstrated on the accompanying recording.

Topics include:
- Basic information on tuning, reading music and reading tablature
- Power chords and rhythm guitar
- Picking techniques and exercises
- Chord voicings for the rock style and rock sound
- Stylistic major scales, minor scales, lead licks and patterns
- Rock lead techniques such as bending, vibrato, double stops, and sequences
- Playing with a band

Also included are play-along tracks featuring legendary recording artists: Tim Bogert on Bass and Tommy Brechtlein on Drums. These tracks enable you to instantly apply the new rhythms, techniques and licks to music.

Two companion videos are also available: Rock Guitar Step 1 (REH869) and Step 2 (REH875)

Parts of the Guitar

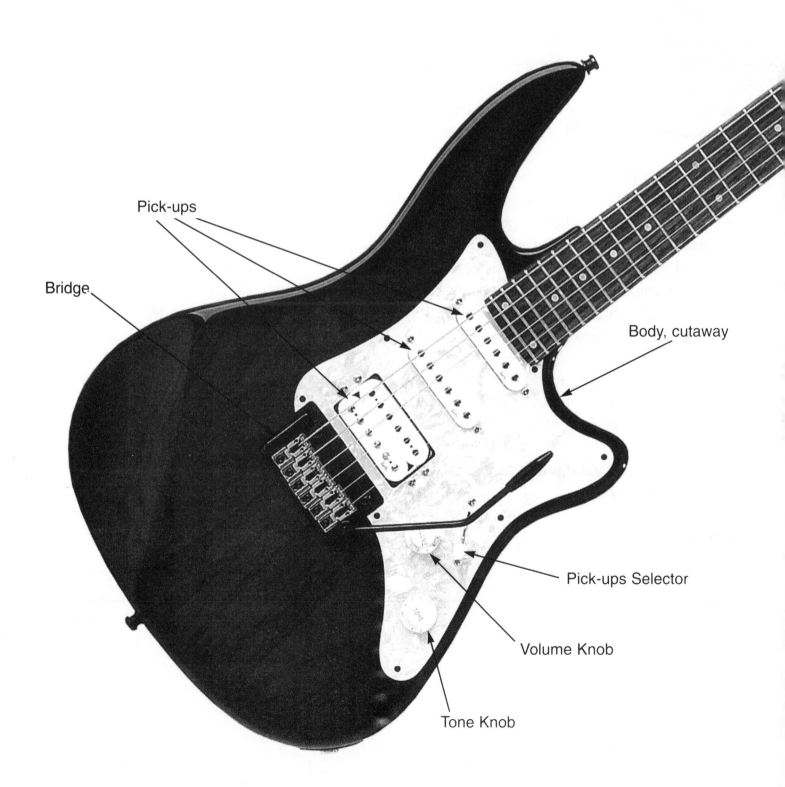

Pick-ups

Bridge

Body, cutaway

Pick-ups Selector

Volume Knob

Tone Knob

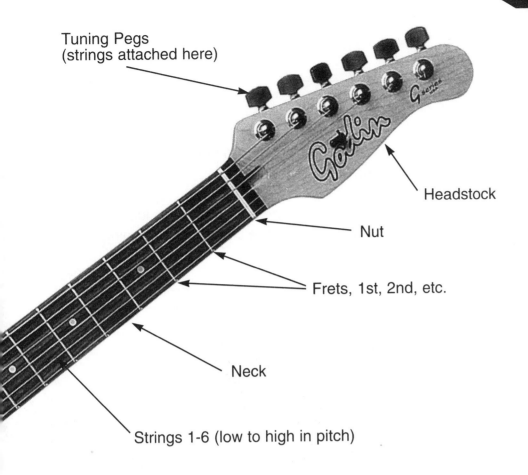

Tuning Pegs
(strings attached here)

Headstock

Nut

Frets, 1st, 2nd, etc.

Neck

Strings 1-6 (low to high in pitch)

Strings: Strings are available in three basic gauges, light, medium and heavy. I suggest you begin with light or medium gauge strings.

Picks: Picks come in many shapes, sizes and thicknesses. For acoustic guitar, I recommend light to medium thickness. For electric, the thicker picks seem to work best. Experiment to find the size and shape you are most comfortable with.

CD

(4) *Tuning Methods*

Tuning to a Keyboard:

The six strings of a guitar can be tuned to a keyboard by matching the sound of each open guitar string to the keyboard notes as indicated in the diagram.

Note: You will hear the intonation better, and your guitar will stay in better tune, if you loosen the strings and tune them **up** to pitch rather than bringing them from above the pitch and tuning down.

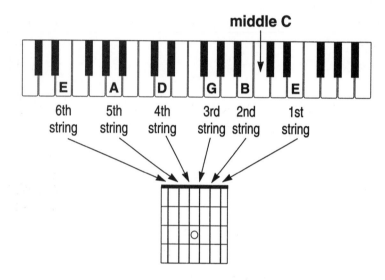

Electronic Tuners:

Many brands of small, battery operated tuners are available. These are excellent for keeping your guitar in perfect tune and for developing your ear to hear intonation very accurately. Simply follow the instructions supplied with the electronic tuner.

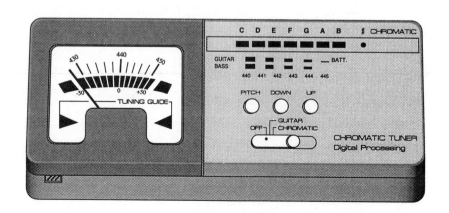

Tuning the Guitar to Itself – The "Fifth Fret" Method:

1) Tune your 6th string "E" to a piano or some other fixed pitch instrument.

2) Depress the 6th string at the 5th fret. Play it and you will hear the note "A," which is the same as the 5th string played open. Turn the 5th string tuning key until the pitch of the open 5th string (A) matches that of the 6th string/5th fret (also A).

3) Depress the 5th string at the 5th fret. Play it and you will hear the note "D," which is the same as the 4th string played open. Turn the 4th string tuning key until the pitch of the open 4th string (D) matches that of the 5th string/5th fret (also D).

4) Depress the 4th string at the 5th fret. Play it and you will hear the note "G," which is the same as the 3rd string played open. Turn the 3rd string tuning key until the pitch of the open 3rd string (G) matches that of the 4th string/5th fret (also G).

5) Depress the 3rd string at the 4th fret (not the 5th fret as in the other strings). Play it and you will hear the note "B," which is the same as the 2nd string played open. Turn the 2nd string tuning key until the pitch of the open 2nd string (B) matches that of the 3rd string/4th fret (also B).

6) Depress the 2nd string at the 5th fret. Play it and you will hear the note "E," which is the same as the 1st string played open. Turn the 1st string tuning key until the pitch of the open 1st string (E) matches that of the 2nd string/5th fret (also E).

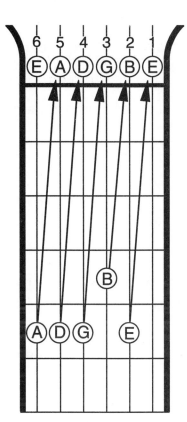

Reading Rhythm Notation

At the beginning of every song is a time signature. 4/4 is the most common time signature:

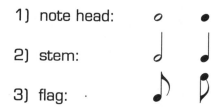

4   FOUR COUNTS TO A MEASURE

4   A QUARTER NOTE RECEIVES ONE COUNT

The top number tells you how many counts per measure.
The bottom number tells you which kind of note receives one count.

The time value of a note is determined by three things:

1) note head: o   •

2) stem:

3) flag:

o   This is a whole note. The note head is open and has no stem. In 4/4 time, a whole note receives 4 counts.

This is a half note. It has an open note head and a stem. A half note receives 2 counts.

This is a quarter note. It has a solid note head and a stem. A quarter note receives 1 count.

This is an eighth note. It has a solid note head and a stem with a flag attached. An eighth note receives 1/2 count.

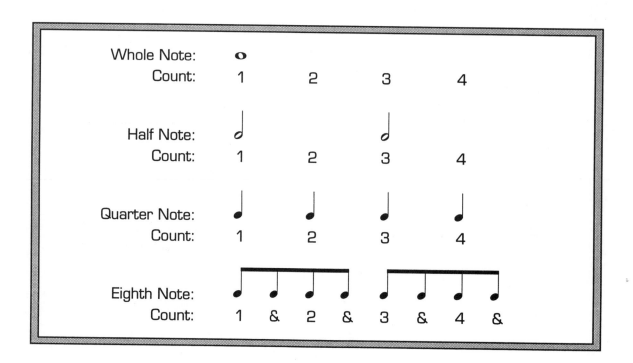

Reading Music Notation

Music is written on a **staff**. The staff consists of five lines and four spaces between the lines:

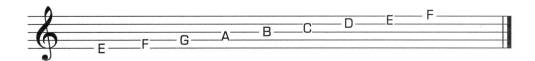

The names of the notes are the same as the first seven letters of the alphabet: A B C D E F G.

The notes are written in alphabetical order. The first (lowest) line is "E":

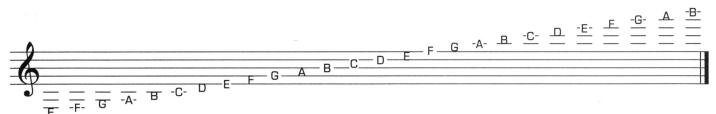

Notes can extend above and below the staff. When they do, **ledger lines** are added. Here is the approximate range of the guitar from the lowest note, open 6th string "E," to a "B" on the 1st string at the 17th fret.

The staff is divided into **measures** by **bar lines**. A heavy double bar line marks the end of the music.

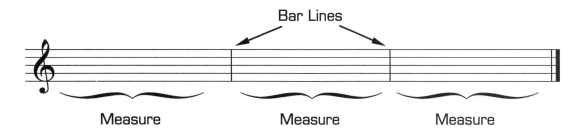

Reading Tablature and Fretboard Diagrams

Tablature illustrates the location of notes on the neck of the guitar. This illustration compares the six strings of a guitar to the six lines of tablature.

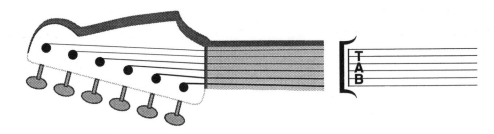

Notes are indicated by placing fret numbers on the strings. An "O" indicates an open string.

This tablature indicates to play the open, 1st and 3rd frets on the 1st string.

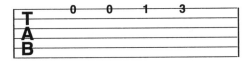

Tablature is usually used in conjunction with standard music notation. The rhythms and note names are indicated by the standard notation and the location of those notes on the guitar neck is indicated by the tablature.

Chords are often indicated in **chord block diagrams**. The vertical lines represent the strings and the horizontal lines represent the frets. Scales are often indicated with guitar **fretboard diagrams**. Here the strings are horizontal and the frets are vertical.

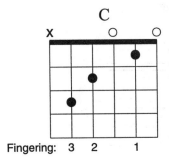

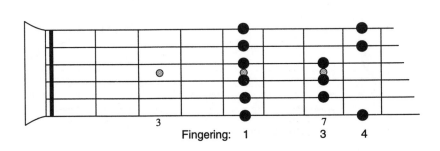

SECTION 2: POWER CHORDS & RHYTHM PLAYING

CD ③ *Barre Chords*

Let's review the movable G and C barre chords. Major chords have three notes; the root, 3rd and 5th. For example:

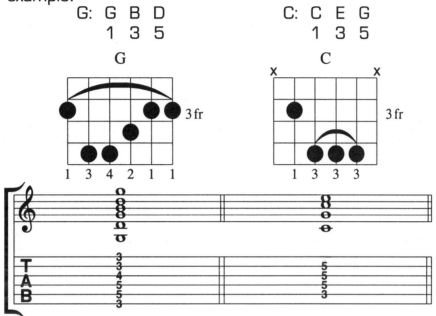

CD ④ *Power Chords*

The rock guitarist's main chord is often called the "**power chord**." The symbols for these chords are either '5' or (no 3rd): C5, G5, D5 or C(no3rd), G(no3rd), etc. These are two-note chords containing only the root and 5th:

G5: G D   C5: C G
    1 5   1 5

Barre chords and open chords sound great with a clean sound but do not always sound so great when you turn on the distortion. Power chords work perfectly with distortion because they have only two different notes.

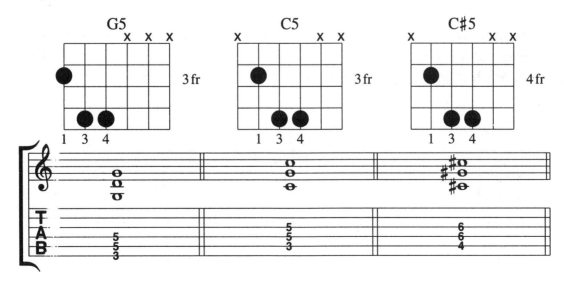

Open Postion Power Chords

It is important to memorize the open power chords. Notice the dead strings on the G5 and the C5 (C5 is not on recording). This is accomplished by allowing the second finger to lightly touch the string while it plays a note on a lower string. This is a valuable technique for cleaning up your distorted sound that will carry over into other areas of your technique.

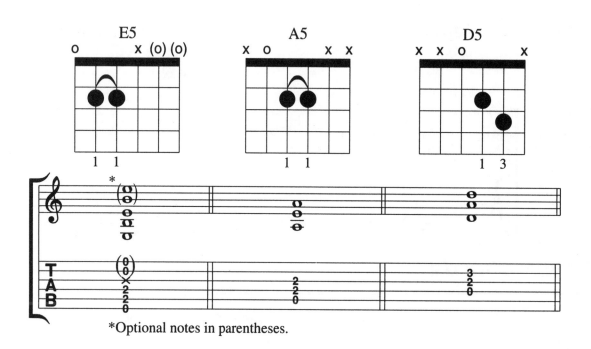

*Optional notes in parentheses.

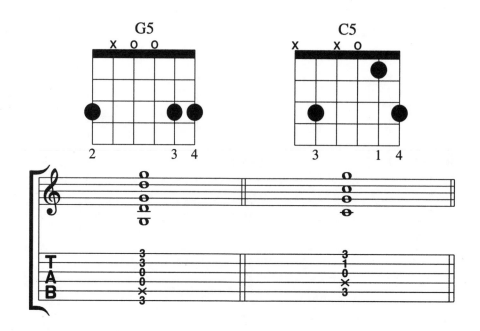

CD 6

Example 1: Right Hand Rhythm Technique

Palm muting (P.M.) adds variety and control to both a distorted and clean sound. You accomplish this technique by lightly placing the palm of your picking hand on the string either on the bridge or slightly in front of the bridge while striking the notes or chords. Avoid placing your hand too far in front of the bridge or the strings will be too muted. Vary the amount of pressure to create a variety of attacks. The palm mute effect is indicated by the abbreviation: **P.M.**

Using all down strokes for rhythm can add a heavier edge to the sound. Use all down strokes and palm muting for Examples 1 & 2.

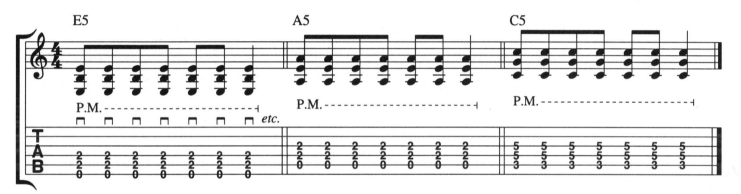

CD 7

Example 2

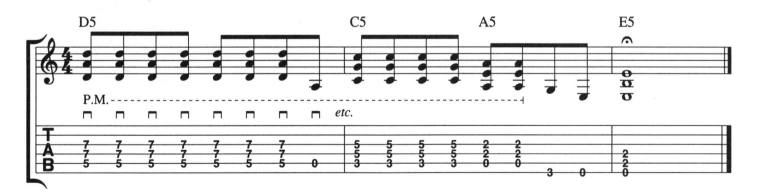

CD 8

Example 3: Power Chord Test (Play-Along Track 1)

It is very important that you memorize each chord you learn. As an exercise, cover up the tablature and use the chord symbols while playing along with the recording. Only refer to the tablature if something doesn't sound right. When you perform with others, you are not likely to have tablature provided. Chord names may be called out to you or you will be given a chord chart.

POWER CHORD TEST
(Play-Along Track 1)

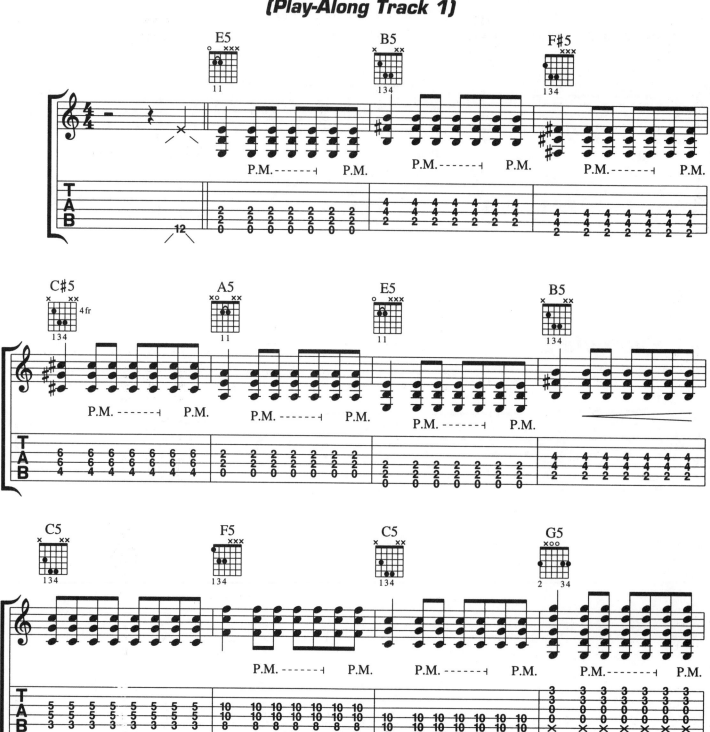

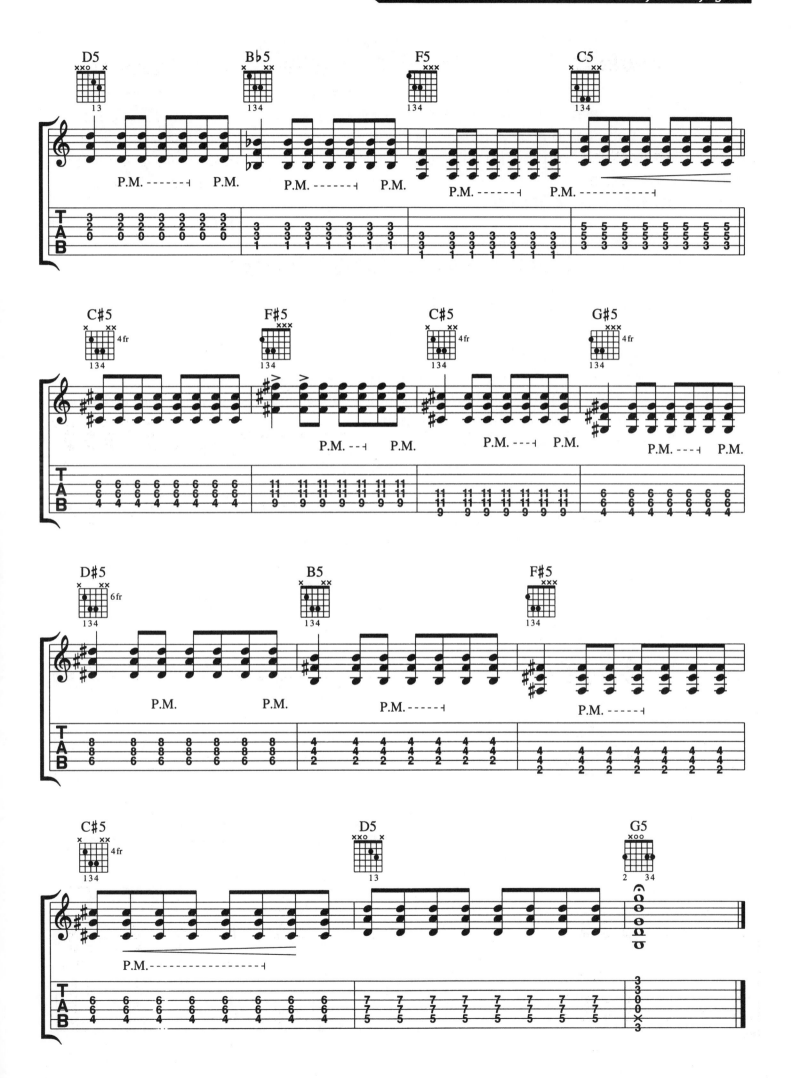

SECTION 3: MORE CHORDS

The following chords will sound better without distortion. If you do use distortion, palm muting and arpeggiation will reduce the harshness. **Arpeggiation** is playing the chord one note at a time, a useful technique for both rhythm and lead.

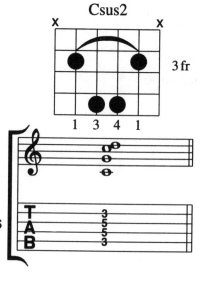

CD 9 *The Csus2 Chord*

The sus2 chord is an extension of the power chord. As the name states, you add the 2nd note of the scale to the chord. The 2nd note of a C scale is D. Depending on how the notes of these chords are arranged, you can also call them add2, add9, or (9) chords.

CD 10 *The 'Sus4' Chord*

The suspended chord (sus), also known as the sus4 chord, replaces the 3rd with a 4th resulting in a chord consisting of a root, 4th and 5th.

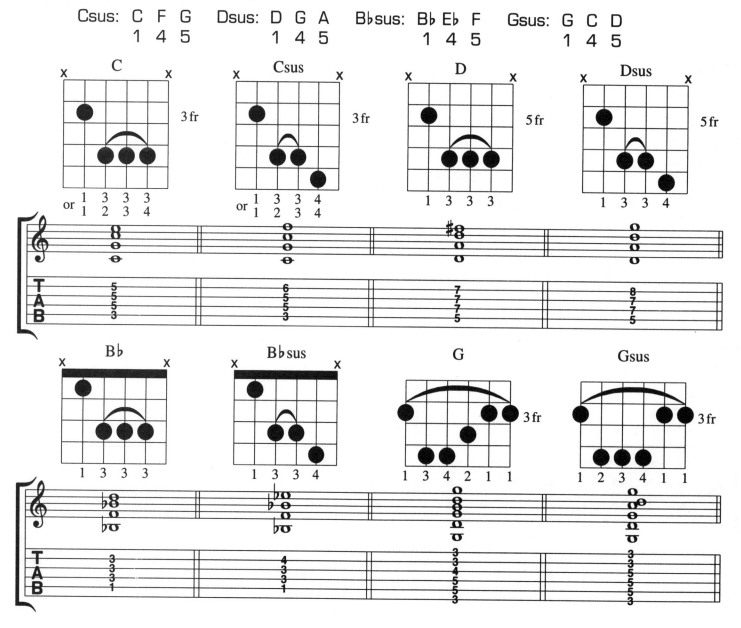

CD
(11) *Example 4: Power Jam (Play-Along Track 2)*

The best way to master any technique or skill is to apply it to music. If you can't find existing musical examples, write your own. This progression is designed to help you practice all of the chords that you have learned so far: sus2, sus4 and movable and open position power chords.

POWER JAM

(Play-Along Track 2)

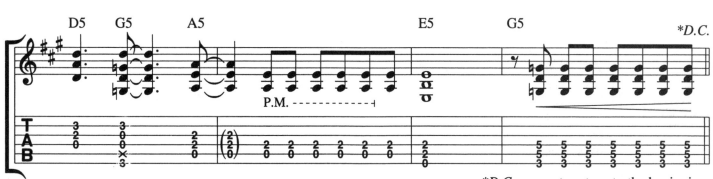

*D.C. means to return to the beginning.

SECTION 4: ROCK LICKS

CD 12

Example 5: The Minor Pentatonic Scale

The most common rock scale is the minor pentatonic. This scale is a five-tone scale that implies a minor harmony. The lowest note of the following fingering is the root of the scale. Since this root is on A this scale is called the A minor pentatonic. Since the root is played with the first finger on the E string (sixth string), it is called the 1E fingering.

The A Minor Pentatonic Scale 1E Fingering

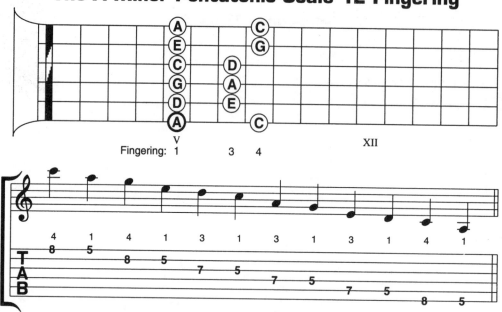

CD 13

Example 6: Changing Key

Like barre chords, scale fingerings are movable. If for example, you play the 1E pentatonic fingering two frets higher you would have a B minor pentatonic scale. Take some time to play and memorize all of the remaining keys while making sure that you pay close attention to what note the root is.

The B Minor Pentatonic Scale 1E Fingering

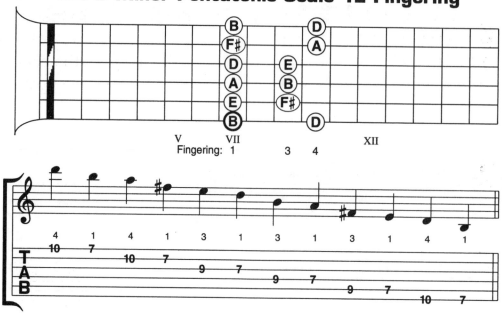

BENDING

The techinque of stretching the string to a higher note is called **bending**. It is very important that you make every attempt to bend the note all the way to the proper pitch; you can't be sharp or flat, you have to be right on target. Having good, accurate bends is essential for any lead guitarist. Let's review the things to remember when bending:

- Use as many fingers as possible. If you're bending with your fourth finger, make sure the other three are right behind it. If you're bending with your third finger, support it with the first and second finger. If you're bending with your second finger, support it with your first finger. The first finger is on its own.

- When bending upward, some people wrap their thumb over the top of the neck for support.

- Make sure you are bending accurately to pitch by comparing the bent note to a fretted note.

CD
(14) *Example 7: Bending Lick*

Remember to use as many fingers as available for strength and support. If, like the first note of this lick, you bend a note with your 3rd finger, use your 1st and 2nd fingers to help support the bend.

This lick starts off with a bend from the D on the 3rd string, 7th fret to the E which, if the note is bent correctly, will sound like the 9th fret of the same string. So that your ear knows how far you have to bend, strike an E first, bend the D until it sounds correct, then check yourself by playing the E again. You might find it easier to check the bent note against the E on the 5th fret of the 2nd string since that is the E that follows the bend in the lick.

CD 15

Example 8: Bending Exercise

Here's an exercise that will help you improve your bending precision. Using bends only, play through a C major scale on the 3rd string. You will probably recognize the do, re, mi, fa, sol, la, ti, do characteristic of the major scale. There are two places that you have a short bend (half step): between the E and F and between the B and C. Be careful to avoid bending too far.

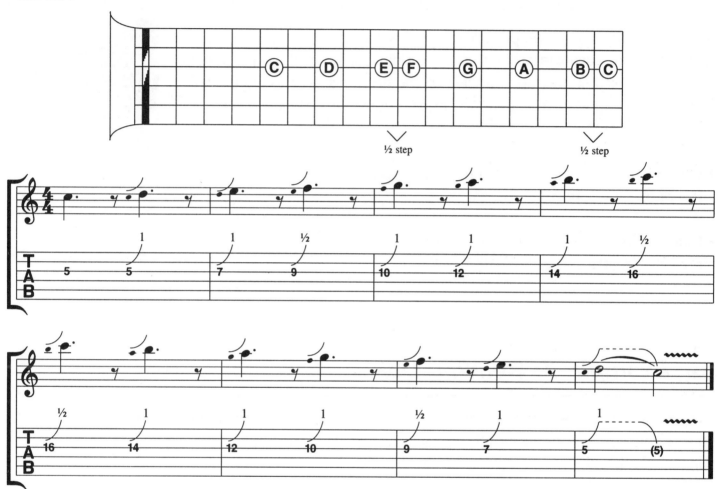

CD 16

Example 9: Minor Pentatonic Bends

In the minor pentatonic scale some notes seem to be bent more often than others. While this does not mean that you have any hard and fast rules about which notes are bent, you should use the following chart to organize your bending ideas.

This diagram illustrates the three most commonly bent notes in the minor pentatonic scale.

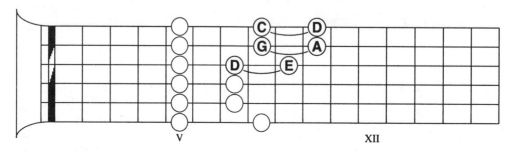

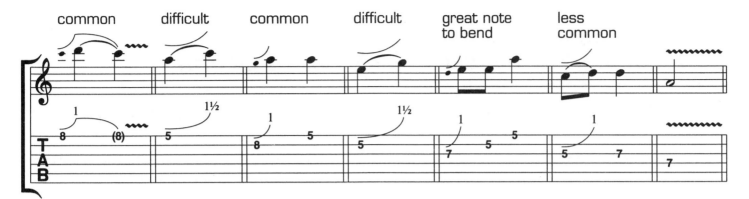

Vibrato:

As the word implies, you can describe vibrato as "vibrating" the notes you play. You can also think of it as a series of tiny bends that make the notes you play have more feeling and emotion. This is a technique often used to make an instrument sound more like a singer's voice. Vibrato is quite often the most identifiable characteristic of a guitar player's style.

The most important aspect of vibrato is evenness, both in distance and in rhythm. How far you bend the string is something that your ear will establish but you have to make sure you bend the string the same distance each time. Sometimes you might prefer a wider vibrato and other times you won't; there is nothing wrong with this as long as your vibrato is always even.

There are many types of vibrato but most rock players use **wrist vibrato**. This is accomplished by bending and releasing the string while making sure that the movement is centered at the wrist.

Some Points to remember:
• Like bending, remember to use as many fingers as available to reinforce the finger that is holding the note.

• Rest the neck of the guitar on the spot where the first finger joins your hand. Use this part of your hand as a fulcrum point. Pivot the wrist back and forth and repeatedly pull the string down (towards the floor) and return. You can also execute a vibrato by pushing upward.

• To move more freely, some people completely release their thumb from the neck.

• Begin with a very slow, wide vibrato and then adjust it according to taste.

CD 18

Example 10: Sequence Lick With Pull-offs

This next lick starts off with a **sequence**. A sequence is an arrangement of notes that repeat.

There are a lot of **pull-offs** in this lick which will help you build up speed sooner. To play a pull-off, place your fingers on the first *two* notes of the lick. Strike the first note and then pull your 4th finger across the string as if you're trying to pluck the string with your fourth finger. Make sure that your first finger does not come off of its note. When you pull the fourth finger off the string, you will be exposing the note that your first finger was holding. This way you only pick one note for every two notes you play.

In addition to the convenience, pull-offs add more style to the lick. Try the same lick with and without the pull-offs to get an idea of how much the sound and feel is affected by the inclusion and exclusion of these slurs. Apply this same type of comparison with the remaining licks in the book.

CD 19

Example 11: Double-Stop Lick

A **double-stop** means playing two notes at the same time. Chuck Berry made this sound popular and now it's a staple riff of almost every guitarist.

CD 20

Example 12: Extended fingerings

You can extend the range of the minor pentatonic scale by shifting from one position to another. You will be playing the same notes as before but locating them on different parts of the neck. Not only does this extend the range of the scale but it allows you more options for fingering. The different fingerings can make licks that are difficult, even unplayable in one position, easier to play by re-arranging the fingerings. For example, you can not execute a true pull-off between notes that are on different strings. The best solution is to find a fingering that places the notes you need on the same string.

A Minor Pentatonic

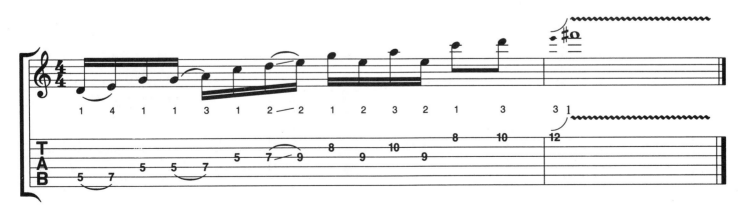

CD 21

Example 13: Extended fingering lick

The following lick is based on the extended fingering.

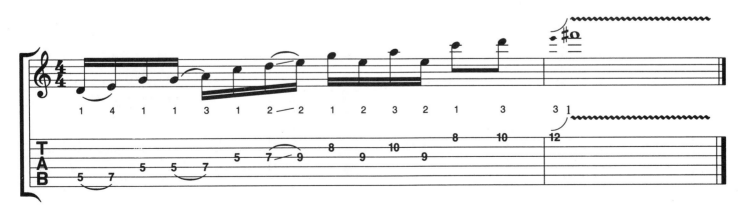

CD 22 *Octaves*

The extended fingering contains the same notes as the box fingering but on different strings and different octaves. It is important that you eventually learn all of the different locations for each note.

The following diagram shows all of the possible locations for the note A. The important thing that you should notice is the distance between each of the notes. These distances create visual shapes that are easy to memorize. It is much easier to get around the fingerboard if you memorize the following, movable octave *shapes* and then apply them to the remaining eleven notes:

Octave Diagram

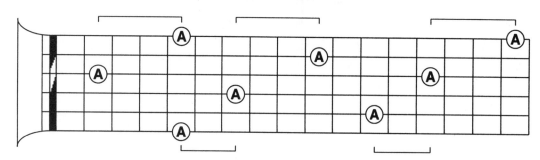

Octave Shapes

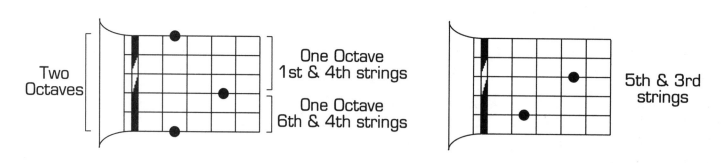

Two Octaves — One Octave 1st & 4th strings / One Octave 6th & 4th strings

5th & 3rd strings

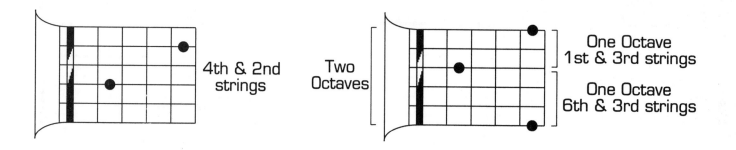

4th & 2nd strings

Two Octaves — One Octave 1st & 3rd strings / One Octave 6th & 3rd strings

Example 14: New Scale Fingering

When you play a scale within a four or five fret range you are playing a box position. The following fingering is a box position for the A minor pentatonic scale on the twelfth fret. This time the root of the scale is under the first finger on the lowest note on the 5th string. This fingering is sometimes called the 1A fingering because you are playing the lowest root with the 1st finger on the A string.

A Minor Pentatonic 1A Fingering

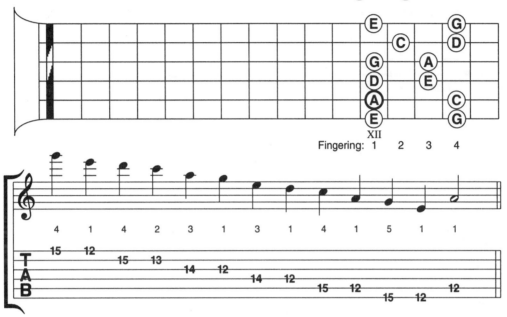

Example 15

The following example is based on the 1A fingering. Notice some previously discussed devices: bending, double-stops and a pull-off. The second measure introduces a hammer-on which is the opposite of the pull-off. You play a lower note on one string and add a higher note on the same string by "hammering" your finger down on to the fret. You do not have to hit the higher note very hard but you do have to move quickly to keep the string vibrating. If you move too slow you will kill the vibration of the string.

When playing the bend combined with the double-stop, you have to be very careful to bend only the note on the second string. Your 4th finger should hold the note on the 1st string without bending it.

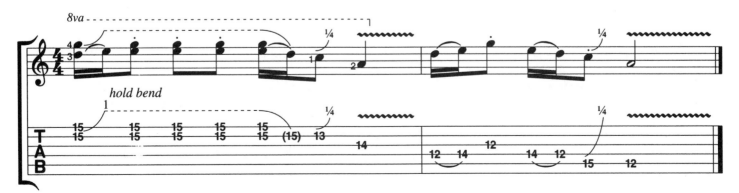

CD
(25) *Example 16: Picking Exercise*

As you learn more and more licks you will find that some are more demanding than others. What you need to do is work on some exercises to get your two hands working together.

Use the following repetitive picking exercise to help build your picking accuracy. Make sure you play each note separately and do not go too fast. Concentrate on making sure you constantly alternate between down-strokes (⊓) and up-strokes (∨). Practice each of the measures separately before you combine them.

CD
(26) *Example 17: Left Hand Hammer*

This lick is another repetitive pattern that combines bending with pull-offs. There is a new technique involving a hammer-on to the 8th fret of the second string which is called the **left hand hammer**. Unlike most hammer-ons, this one is landing on a string that isn't already ringing.

CD
(27) *Example 18: New Sequence Pattern*

Here is a sequence exercise. As with all of the other exercises, this works well as a soloing idea.

CD 28

Example 19: Driving Rock Jam (Play-Along Track 3)

After taking in all of this new information, it would be a great idea to try it all out by jamming with friends or play-along tracks, including the tracks on the recording.

After the solo is over, it is your turn to solo. The progression is in the key of A so it will be easy for you to apply any of the licks and scales that have been covered up to this point.

Try experimenting with mixing ideas from different parts of the neck. For example, try starting something in the A minor pentatonic, 5th position (1E fingering):

Example 19A

"And then move on up to the minor pentatonic in the 12 position" (1A fingering):

Example 19B

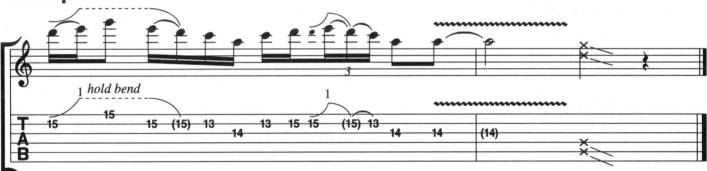

CD 29

Example 19C: Play-Along

The solo has been transcribed note for note to provide you with more ideas. Make sure that you try to identify the scales and the fingering and that you listen carefully to how the harmony affects whatever idea you learn. You will probably recognize that the progression is the same as the one you learned in Example 4. Accompany the solo using that example.

DRIVING ROCK JAM
(Play-Along Track 3)

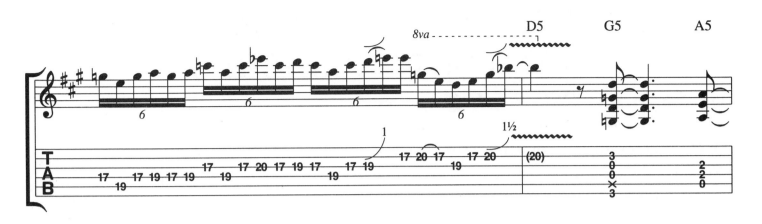

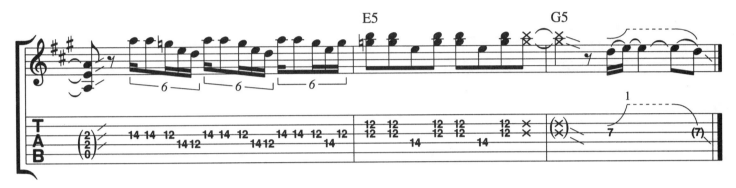

Driving Rock Jam Progression

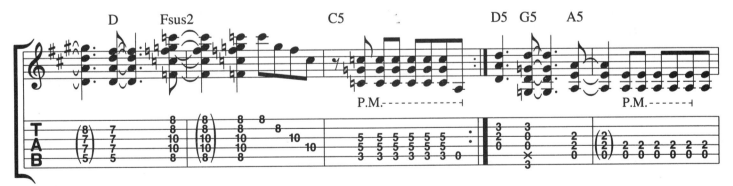

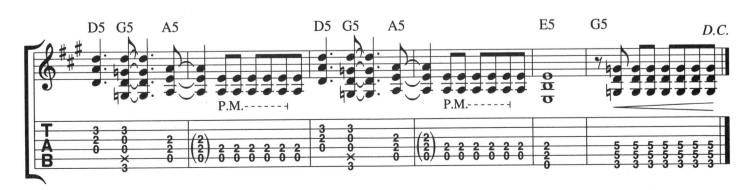

SECTION 5: DOMINANT 7 AND MINOR 7 CHORDS

CD 30 *Example 20: Funk Groove*

The following example is a rhythm figure demonstrating a funky groove using thicker harmonies than the previous rhythms covered in this book. Again, notice that with distortion you risk the sound becoming cluttered if you are not careful.

CD 31 *Dominant 7 chords*

Let's review dominant 7th chords. These chords are abundant in blues, funk, rock, metal, alternative, country and southern rock. Dominant 7 chords have a root, 3rd, 5th and 7th.

G7: G B D F
1 3 5 ♭7

C7: C E G B♭
1 3 5 ♭7

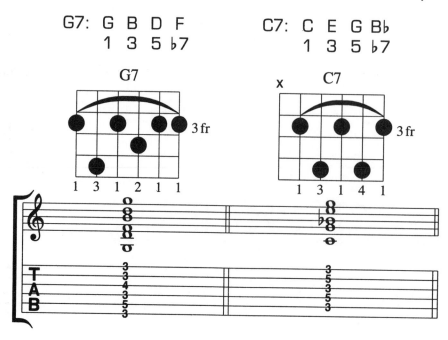

CD
(32) *Minor 7 chords*

Compare the previous dominant fingerings to these minor 7th voicings. Minor 7 chords have a root, ♭3rd, 5th and ♭7th.

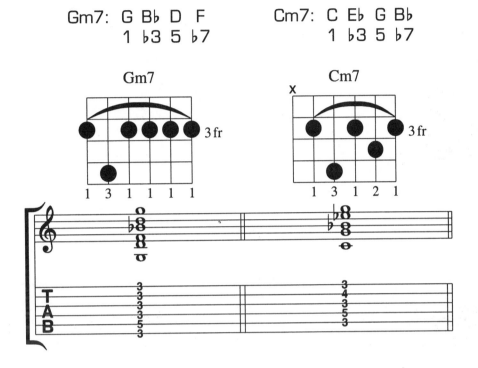

Gm7: G B♭ D F
       1 ♭3 5 ♭7

Cm7: C E♭ G B♭
       1 ♭3 5 ♭7

CD
(33) *"Emptied Out" Fingerings*

Both the dominant and minor 7th chords have a harmonically rich sound; too rich for distortion except in special circumstances. As stated before, you can reduce the "muddy" distortion by reducing the number of notes in the chords. The 5th is an expendable note. With your distorted sound, compare the following fingerings, which omit the 5th, with the previous examples.

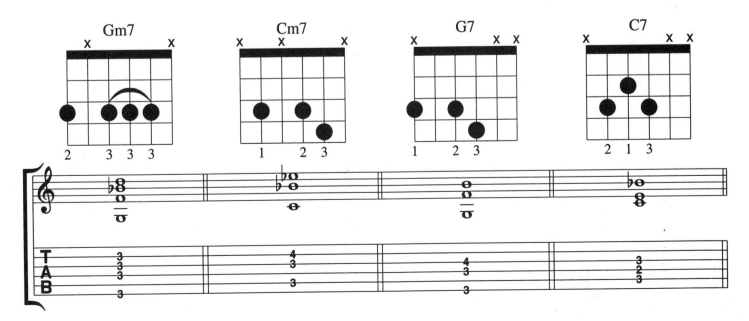

CD 34 *Example 21*

Play the full voicing using the clean sound and switch to the "emptied out" version using the distortion.

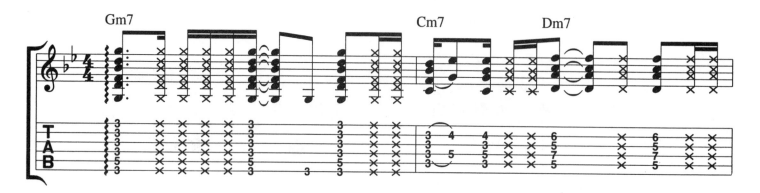

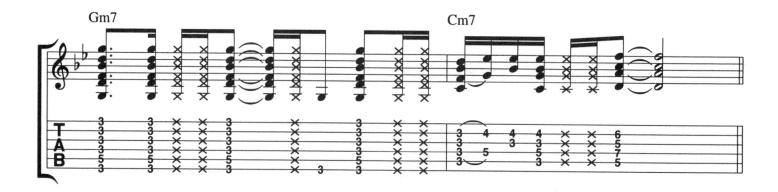

Now add distortion.

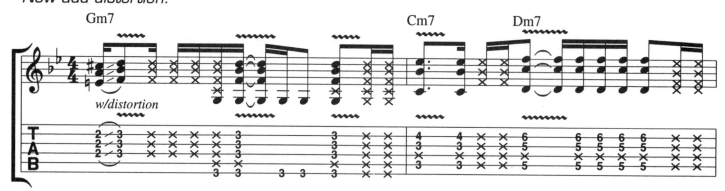

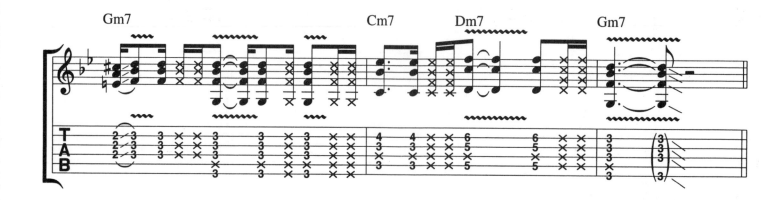

CD 35 *Example 22: Minor Funk Jam (Play-Along Track 4)*

The following progression contains examples of "emptied out" voicings of minor 7 and dominant 7 chords and examples of add2 chords.

MINOR FUNK JAM
(Play-Along Track 4)

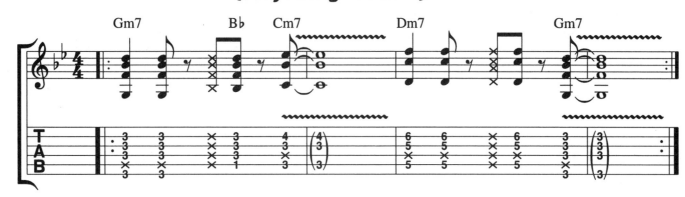

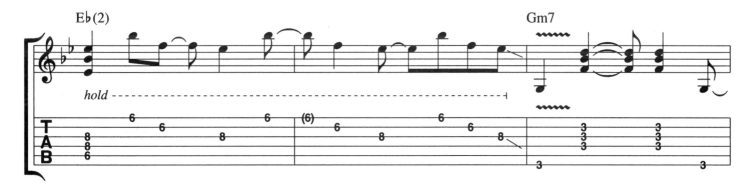

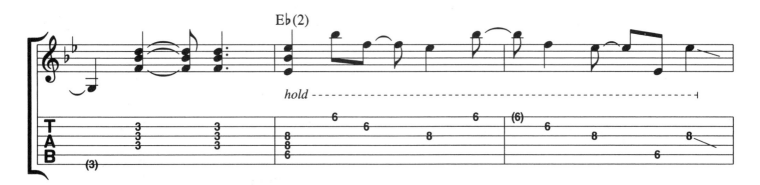

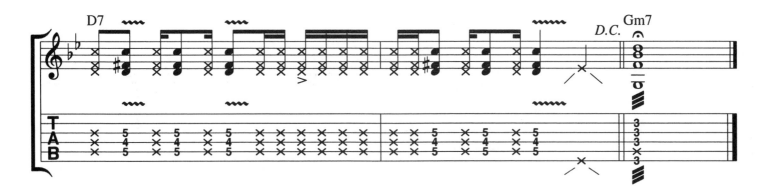

Example 23: Mixing Single Lines With Chords

Let's take the next step, as far as rhythm guitar goes, and approach the chords a bit differently. Instead of just strumming through them, break them up. Hit the lowest note first, stop it, and then hit the upper part. Practice this pattern slowly to make sure that there's separation between the low and high notes. Mute the low note while leaving the upper notes unmuted for better separation.

Example 23A

Example 23B

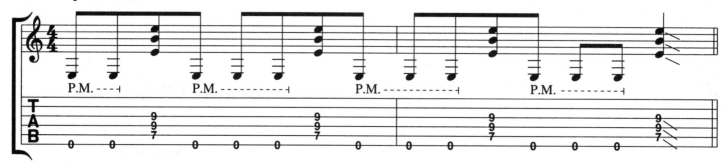

Example 23C

Example 24: Pedal Tone Progression

Try putting different chords together with the open E. The open E is called a pedal tone. While pedaling on the E, experiment with different chords using your ear to determine which ones you like.

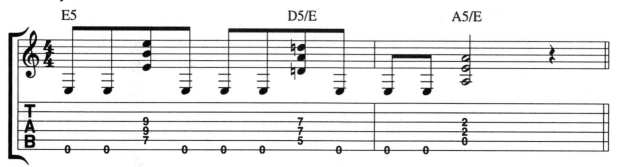

Example 25: Pedal to the Metal (Play-Along Track 5)

The following progression provides examples of pedaling and demonstrates single line accompaniment. Notice the usage of "emptied out" fingerings for the minor 7 and dominant 7 chords.

PEDAL TO THE METAL
(Play-Along Track 5)

SECTION 6: PICKING TECHNIQUES

CD
(39) *Example 26*

For most people, the hardest thing to master about picking technique is getting the two hands to work together. It's kind of easy to go fast, but to be accurate about it with both hands is another thing. The following exercises are designed to syncronize your hands. Your goal is to make each note sound separated and clear. The worst thing you can do is go for speed right away. Play each note slowly, firmly and clearly with strict alternate picking. Also move each exercise to different strings and positions.

Example 26A

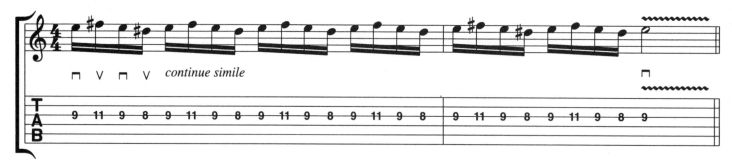

Example 26B

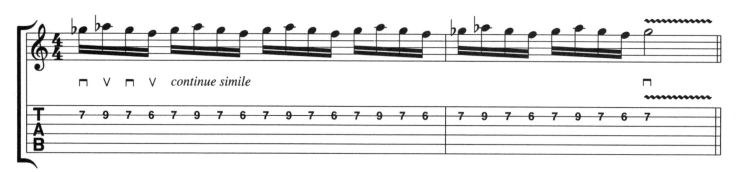

Example 26C

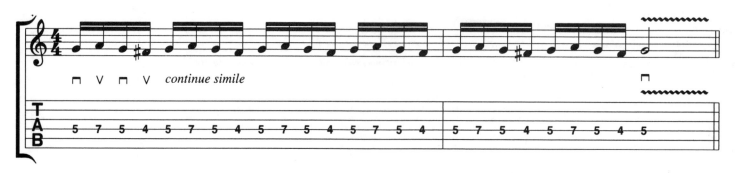

Example 27: String Switching

Examples 27A-27C focus on string switching. String switching is often a challenge for the right hand especially if you are using alternate picking.

Example 27A

Example 27B

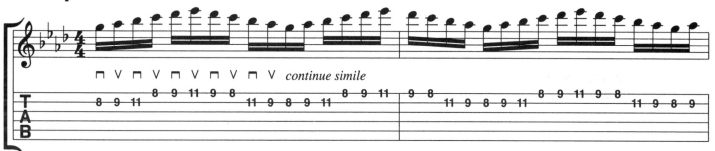

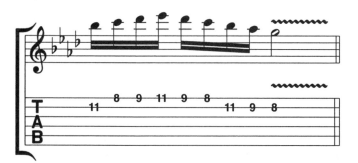

Example 27C

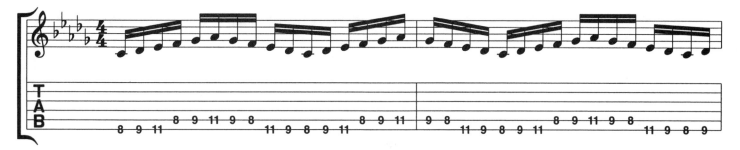

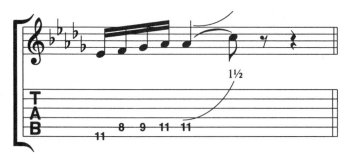

CD
41

Example 28: Hammer-ons and Pull-offs

Now add hammer-ons and pull-offs while maintaining a separated and clear sound. A hammer-on is the opposite of a pull-off: play the first note with your pick, sound the next note by hammering your second finger onto the string without striking it.

Example 28A

Example 28B

Example 28C

By combining Examples 28A and 28B you have a lick that works really well for soloing.

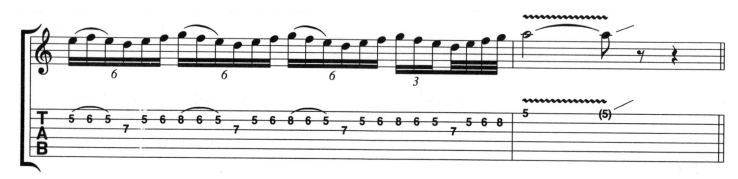

SECTION 7:
MAJOR PENTATONIC SCALES

Up to now, all of our licks have come from the minor pentatonic scale; in this case the B minor pentatonic. But B minor is not the only name for this scale, it's also called the D major pentatonic scale. Every minor scale has a relative major and vice versa. The easiest way to remember the difference is that on the sixth string, the note under your first finger is the minor root and the fourth finger is on the major root.

The D Major Pentatonic Scale 4E Fingering

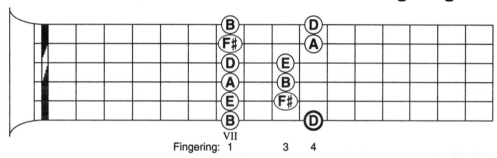

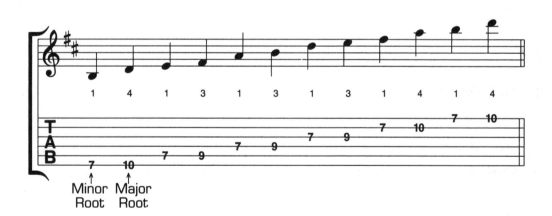

Songs are basically in a major key or a minor key. If you play a song that's in D major then you need a scale that works for D major.

What defines a scale in a major key? Setting aside complicated theoretical explanations, the basic rule to remember is that if the "home" chord is a major chord then you are most likely in a major key. The home chord is usually the chord that starts and finishes the progression.

CD **43** **Example 29: Major Jam (Play-Along Track 6)**

Most of the minor pentatonic licks that you've learned so far can work as relative major pentatonic, but you should resolve on the root. Notice the following progression starts and ends on a D chord. As a result, D major pentatonic would be a good choice. Notice how the D note connects the scale to the chord.

MAJOR JAM
(Play-Along Track 6)

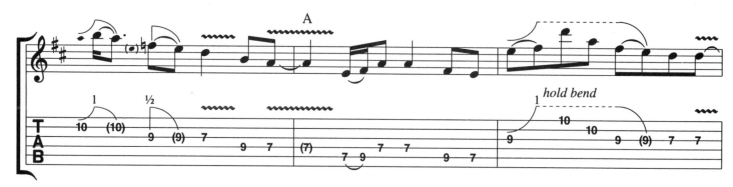

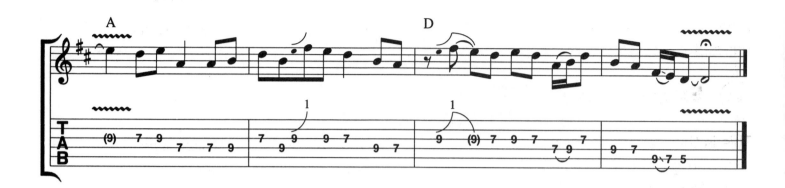

"Now try your own solo, using the D major pentatonic scale, over the following progression."

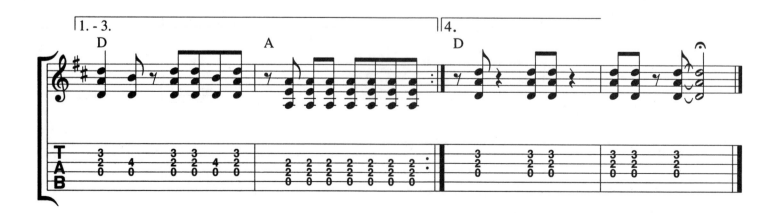

SECTION 8: DIATONIC SCALES

Diatonic scales are seven-note scales; two more than the pentatonic, and they are the basis of almost all the music we listen to.

 44 *Example 30: A Minor Scale*

This is the diatonic A minor scale, which is usually called A minor, A natural minor or A pure minor. A great way to learn the A minor scale is to take the A minor pentatonic scale and add a 2nd (B) and a 6th (F).

A minor: A B C D E F G A   A minor pentatonic: A C D E G A
         1 2 ♭3 4 5 ♭6 ♭7 1   1 ♭3 4 5 ♭7 1

The A minor scale is relative to the C major scale; they have the same notes but start on different roots.

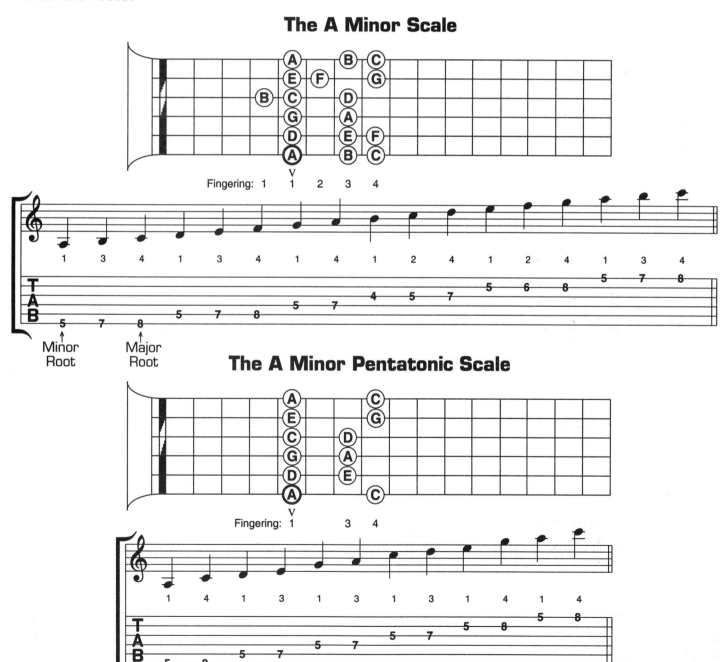

The A Minor Scale

The A Minor Pentatonic Scale

Example 31: Minor Jam (Play-Along Track 7)

The following solo uses the complete A minor scale, notice the inclusion of the B and F and their effect.

MINOR JAM
(Play-Along Track 7)

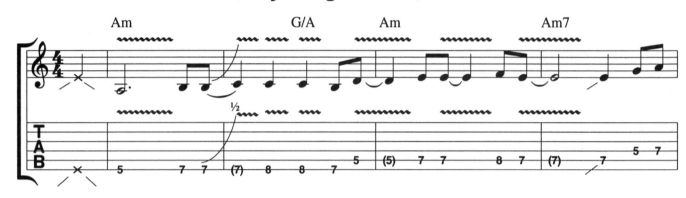

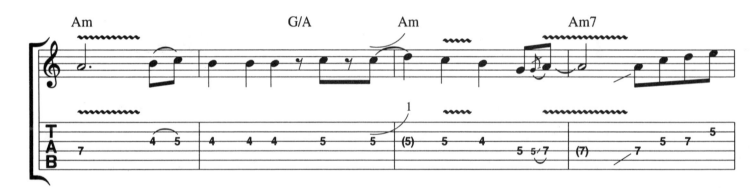

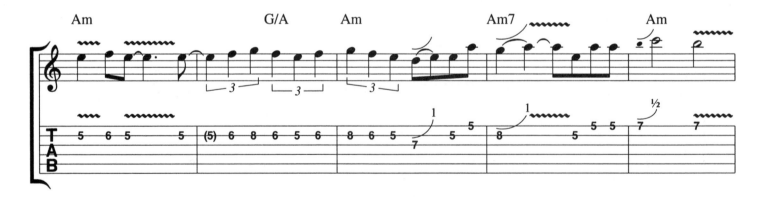

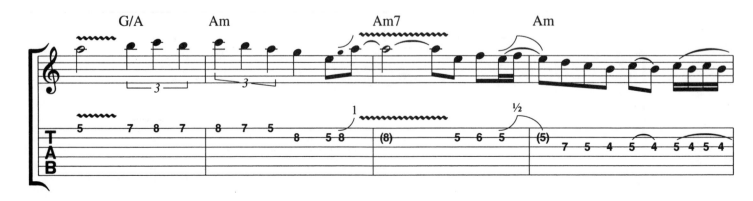

"Now try your own solo, using the A minor scale over this progression."

SECTION 9: NEW LICKS

CD 46 *Example 32: A Minor Pentatonic*

Try to approach this lick as an A minor lick, and then try to hear it as an A minor pentatonic scale with the B and F added.

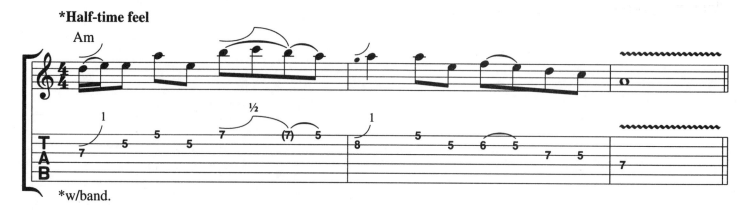

Example 33: A Minor

This A minor lick employs pull-offs, a sequence and then a combination of a bend and release to a pull-off. Since it resolves to A, it sounds like an A minor lick.

CD 47 **Example 33A**

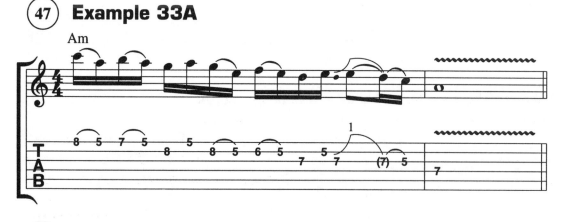

CD 48 **Example 33B: C Major**

If you want to make Example 33A a C major lick, make your last note C.

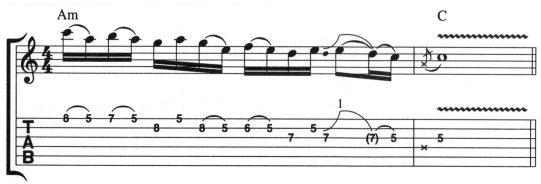

CD 49

Example 34: Three-Note-Per-String Fingering

Remember that patterns and fingerings are a convenience not a rule. Sometimes it is easier to "displace" a couple of notes. Here the C that is usually played on the 6th string is displaced to the 5th string, and the 5th string F is played on the 4th string. By adding a G to the 6th string, you end up with three-notes-per-string which makes it convenient for rhythmic patterns and slur patterns.

Three-Note-Per-String Scale

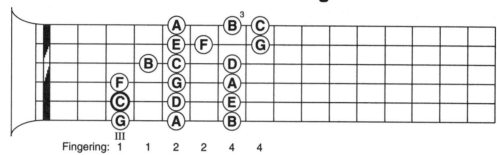

CD 50

Example 35: Three-Note-Per-String Lick

CD 51

WRAP UP

Where do you go from here? One thing is to keep listening to your favorite guitarists. If you can, find a good teacher. There are also plenty of good books and videos, but nothing will replace the experience of playing with other musicians. Get together with your friends and jam a lot or even write your own tunes. Good luck!

GUITAR TAB GLOSSARY **

TABLATURE EXPLANATION

READING TABLATURE: Tablature illustrates the six strings of the guitar. Notes and chords are indicated by the placement of fret numbers on a given string(s).

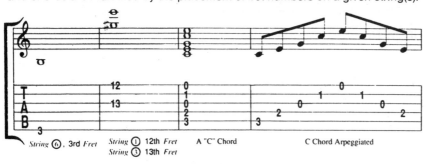

String ⑥, 3rd Fret   String ① 12th Fret   A "C" Chord   C Chord Arpeggiated
String ③ 13th Fret

BENDING NOTES

HALF STEP: Play the note and bend string one half step.*

WHOLE STEP: Play the note and bend string one whole step.

PREBEND AND RELEASE: Bend the string, play it, then release to the original note.

RHYTHM SLASHES

STRUM INDICATIONS: Strum with indicated rhythm.

The chord voicings are found on the first page of the transcription underneath the song title.

INDICATING SINGLE NOTES USING RHYTHM SLASHES: Very often single notes are incorporated into a rhythm part. The note name is indicated above the rhythm slash with a fret number and a string indication.

*A half step is the smallest interval in Western music; it is equal to one fret. A whole step equals two frets.

**By Kenn Chipkin and Aaron Stang

ARTICULATIONS

HAMMER ON: Play lower note, then "hammer on" to higher note with another finger. Only the first note is attacked.

PULL OFF: Play higher note, then "pull off" to lower note with another finger. Only the first note is attacked.

LEGATO SLIDE: Play note and slide to the following note. (Only first note is attacked).

PALM MUTE: The note or notes are muted by the palm of the pick hand by lightly touching the string(s) near the bridge.

ACCENT: Notes or chords are to be played with added emphasis.

DOWN STROKES AND UPSTROKES: Notes or chords are to be played with either a downstroke (⊓·) or upstroke (∨) of the pick.

© 1990 Beam Me Up Music
c/o CPP/Belwin, Inc. Miami, Florida 33014
International Copyright Secured   Made in U.S.A.   All Rights Reserved